The Effects of the Doctrine of Discovery

Presented by

Meru El Muad'Dib

AMER'ICAN, noun A native of **America**; originally applied to the **aboriginals**, or **copper-colored** races, found here by the Europeans; but now applied to the descendants of Europeans born in **America**. 1828 Webster's Dictionary

What Is The Doctrine of Discovery?

In case you haven't had the opportunity to read Volume I or II of this series, here is a quick review on what the Doctrine of Discovery is and some of the things it accomplished.

European nations assumed that they had a right to govern the Indian nations they encountered. This right stemmed from the legal and religious **Doctrine of Discovery which declares that Christian nations have a right, if not an obligation, to govern all non-Christian nations**. **Once an Indian nation had been read the Christian history of the world, even though it might be read to them in a language they did not understand, then they were obligated to be ruled by the superior Christian nation**.

The Catholic Pope in 1452 laid the foundation for the Doctrine of Discovery by issuing the papal bull Dum Diversas which instructed the Portuguese monarchy:

*"to invade, capture, vanquish, and subdue all Saracens,**(Moors, Muslims)** pagans, and other enemies of Christ, to put them into perpetual slavery, and to take away all their possessions and property."*

A papal bull is a special kind of patent or charter issued by a pope. It is called a "bull" because of the seal (bulla) which was appended to the end of it and served to authenticate the document.

The Doctrine of Discovery provided Europeans with what they viewed as the legal right to claim the Americas. Europeans felt that while non-Christian Indian nations owned the land, the **European nations, as Christian nations, had the right to rule Indian nations. If the Indian nations failed to recognize this right, then the Christian nations could wage a just war against them**.

In 1513, the Doctrine of Discovery was formalized by the Spanish in a document called the "Requirement". The "requirement" or "requerimento" was drawn up by Palacios Rubios, Spain's master jurist, and **provided the legal basis for the Spanish conquest of the Americas**. All Spanish expeditions were required to carry a copy of the document. In the document, King Ferdinand told Native Americans that God had declared that the Pope rules all people, regardless of their law, sect, or belief. This included Christians, Moors, Jews, Gentiles, or any other sect. He asked that the Native Americans come forward of their own free will to convert to Catholicism or

"with the help of God we shall use force against you, declaring war upon you from all sides and with all possible means, and we shall bind you to the yoke of the Church and Their Highnesses; we shall enslave your persons, wives, and sons, sell you or dispose of you as the King sees fit; we shall seize your possessions and harm you as much as we can as disobedient and resisting vassals."

Furthermore, **the Natives who resist are to be held guilty of all resulting deaths and injuries**.

Upon contacting an Indian village, the Spanish conquistadores would read the 'Requirement' which recited the history of the world as they knew it, from the Garden of Eden to the recent discovery. It did not make any difference that the natives might not understand Spanish or Latin, or that they might have their own history of the world. Once the word of the Spanish god was revealed, **a just war could be waged on those who rejected it**.

The idea of a "just war" was based upon the word of Saint Augustine. Under this concept, a just war was one that was waged to right an injustice or wrong by another nation. One of these wrongs, according to the Christian view, was not being Christian. Thus, **if an Indian nation were to fail to let missionaries live and preach among them, then they were committing a "wrong" which would have to be set right through a "just war**."

http://nativeamericannetroots.net/diary/1129

Theological, Political, and Legal Fiction

The Doctrine of Discovery continues to impact Indigenous Peoples throughout the world. The Doctrine of Discovery provided a framework for Christian explorers, in the name of their sovereign, to lay claim to territories uninhabited by Christians.

The Permanent Forum on Indigenous Issues concluded its eleventh session with the approval of a set of nine draft recommendations, highlighted by a text approved on the special theme, the ongoing impact of the Discovery Doctrine on indigenous peoples and the right redress. That fifteenth century Christian principle was denounced throughout the session as **the "shameful" root of all the discrimination and marginalization indigenous peoples faced today.**

The Permanent Forum noted that, while such doctrines of domination and "conquest", including terra nullis and the Regalian doctrine, were promoted as authority for land acquisition, they also encouraged despicable assumptions: that indigenous peoples were "savages", "barbarians", "inferior and uncivilized," among other constructs the colonizers used to subjugate, dominate and exploit the lands, territories and resources of native peoples.

According to the text, signs of such doctrines were still evident in indigenous communities, including in the areas of **health**; **psychological** and **social well-being**; **conceptual** and **behavioral forms of violence against indigenous women**; **youth suicide**; and **the hopelessness that many indigenous peoples experience**, **in particular indigenous youth**.

https://www.un.org/en/development/desa/newsletter/desanews/dialogue/2012/06/3801.html

1. Indigenous Peoples have the oldest living cultures in the world. Three hundred to five hundred million Indigenous Peoples today live in over 72 countries around the world, and they comprise at least 5,000 distinct peoples. **The ways of life, identities, well-being and very existence of Indigenous People are threatened by the continuing effects of colonization and national policies, regulations and laws that attempt to force them to assimilate into the cultures of majoritarian societies**. A fundamental historical basis and legal precedent for these policies and laws is the "Doctrine of Discovery", the idea that **Christians enjoy a moral and legal right based solely on their religious identity to invade and seize indigenous lands and to dominate Indigenous Peoples**.

2. Around the world, **Indigenous Peoples are over-represented in all categories of disadvantage**. In most **indigenous communities people live in poverty without clean water and necessary infrastructure, lacking adequate health care, education, employment and housing**. **Many indigenous communities still suffer the effects of dispossession**, **forced removals from homelands and families, inter-generational trauma and racism**, **the effects of which are manifested in social welfare issues such as alcohol and drug problems, violence and social breakdown**. **Basic health outcomes**

dramatize the disparity in well-being between Indigenous Peoples and European descendants.

3. The patterns of domination and oppression that continue to afflict Indigenous Peoples today throughout the world are found in numerous historical documents such as Papal Bulls, Royal Charters and court rulings. For example, the church documents Dum Diversas (1452) and Romanus Pontifex (1455) called for non-Christian peoples to be invaded, captured, vanquished, subdued, reduced to perpetual slavery and to have their possessions and property seized by Christian monarchs. Collectively, these and other concepts form a paradigm or pattern of domination that is still being used against Indigenous Peoples.

6. Consequently, the current situation of Indigenous Peoples around the world is the result of a **linear program of "legal" precedent**, **originating with the Doctrine of Discovery and codified in contemporary national laws and policies**. **The Doctrine mandated Christian European countries to attack, enslave and kill the Indigenous Peoples they encountered and to acquire all of their assets**. The Doctrine remains the law in various ways in almost all settler societies around the world today. The enormity of the application of this law and the theft of the rights and assets of Indigenous Peoples have led indigenous activists to work to educate the world about this situation and to galvanize opposition to the Doctrine.
https://www.oikoumene.org/en/resources/documents/executive-committee/2012-02/statement-on-the-doctrine-of-discovery-and-its-enduring-impact-on-indigenous-peoples

The following is a quote from a timeline of the Christian European Spanish barbarism that was part of the conquering and depopulating of the Americas, provided by Kenneth Humphreys.

"The plunder of the empires of the Americas was to good purpose—it allowed Spain to finance religious persecution in Europe for over a century. Spanish wars of conquest included laying waste much of the Netherlands and a disastrous attempt to invade England. By destroying diverse cultures in the New World the Christian conquerors were able not only to eradicate civilizations more ancient than their own but also were able to senselessly erase a vibrant artistic legacy and even scientific knowledge. In their stead the Christian adventurers imposed a racist tyranny...."

The absolutism of the DOD **made its way through the Americas bringing disease to Native tribes and peoples**, literally wiping out entire civilizations. In addition, it provided legitimacy for slavery and shipping of Africans to the new world, and the oppression of other ethnic groups. Always it was justified on two major premises; **one, bringing Christianity to the savages and heathens of the New World; and two, the belief that one race had the divine right and superiority to civilize the world and expand their reach**.

Estimates of the pre-Colombian population of the Americas vary but possibly stood at 100 million—one fifth of humanity in 1492. Between 1500 and 1600 the population of the Americas was halved. In Mexico alone, it has been estimated that the pre-conquest population of around 25 million people was reduced within 80 years to about 1.3 million. In Hawai'i, the population was estimated to be as much as 800,000 at the time of contact in 1798. In less than 60 years, less than 100,000 Native Hawaiians remained.

How could this trail of destruction have been denied for so long? More shockingly**, why did post-Columbian America continue the oppression**? **The European settlers arrived in "America" to escape the oppression of the old world and**

the British Empire and then in the 18th and 19th centuries they repeated the exact behavior of their European oppressors. It was justified under a doctrine called Manifest Destiny which upheld the same dogma as the DOD. https://newsmaven.io/indiancountrytoday/archive/the-sordid-influence-of-the-doctrine-of-discovery-mDI-6yAohUOHrNwv9HJ3RA/

There's been a lot of talk lately about the so-called Doctrine of Discovery, originally a **theological fiction** produced in the 1400s, later transformed into a **political fiction** by European heads of state, and then into a **legal fiction** by U.S.

Today it has been dangerously repurposed as popular fiction that serves to revise neo-colonial history, fuel oppressive legal decisions, and assuage majority culture guilt. Left unchallenged, the myths generated pose grave threats to our identities as peoples with inalienable sovereign rights to governance and territory.

Without question the doctrine of discovery is one of the most important tenets of federal Indian law, working in tandem with several other doctrines–trust, plenary power, and reserved rights—to provide the ambiguous and uneven political framework for modern day Indigenous/State relationships. Notwithstanding its general acceptance, the concept has been so misused to distort perceptions of past and present oppression that it should be stricken from the federal government's political and legal vocabulary.

But it is more complicated than just saying the Pope gave European Catholics the rights to colonize and convert. In reality, the absolute denial of Native land rights was replaced less than fifty years later when Charles V, the devoutly religious Spanish emperor, sought the advice of Francisco de Vitoria, a prominent theologian, as to what rights the Spanish could legally and morally claim in the New World. Vitoria, in a clear rebuttal to the Pope and the discovery notion, **declared that Native peoples were the true owners of their lands. He reasoned the Spanish could not claim title through discovery because this action could only be justified where property was ownerless**.

Felix Cohen, a leading architect of federal Indian law, reiterated Vitoria's statement in his well-known *Handbook of Federal Indian Law* (1941), when he wrote that "**even the Pope has no right to partition the property of the Indians, and in the absence of a just war, only the voluntary consent of the aborigines could justify the annexation of their territory**."

So, in fact, the original no-holds barred papal doctrine of the discovery was discarded early on in favor of Vitoria's view of indigenous property rights. Subsequent legal and political relations between Native nations and competing European powers over the following three centuries were generally based on this philosophical understanding of Natives as true landowners. Treaty-making between tribal nations and Europeans, and later the U.S, affirmed that Native peoples were recognized as land-owning nations on par with any other political power.

Had Pope Alexander's original sweeping decree of unlimited Christian domination held sway, there would have been no reason for colonizers to bother with treaties. Furthermore, **contrary to common assumptions that ultimate legal title to occupied Native lands passed upon discovery to European states or the U.S. as successor, the historical record, both written and oral, shows that legal ownership remained with tribal nations**. And for the most part, Native peoples retained legal ownership of their respective territories until such time as they formally ceded their claims to lands in consensual treaty arrangements with one of the competing European states or, later, the American government.

Three classes of evidence—1) the actual political and diplomatic relations between Native nations and Spain, France, Great Britain; 2) the record of the federal government in its dealing with Native peoples as evidenced in treaties, policies, and statutes; and 3) a number of relevant Supreme Court decisions that have addressed the doctrine of discovery–affirm that ownership of the North American continent rested in the hands of indigenous peoples.

This is not to say that injustices were not committed and great swaths of land taken without recourse. We all know too well that this occurred in many cases. However, it is critically important that we remember our history and the over-arching legal basis of our land ownership. Even as other powers sought to vanquish them, Native peoples retained power over their lands, just as they retained sovereignty. **To simply say that the discovery doctrine allowed colonizers to take land without consideration for indigenous property rights is to passively accept a revised history that claims we never had those rights in the first place**.

The same principle applies to the Louisiana Purchase. It was **never** France's to sell to the Americans. As stated earlier, there was no war, and the aborigines never gave voluntary consent for the French to own the area.

In reality, the discovery doctrine (either the papal or the Vitoria version) was only sometimes referenced during much of the colonial period as land was bought, sold, and traded with the understanding that indigenous peoples held ownership rights. But it was famously reprised and redefined by the US Supreme Court in *Johnson v. McIntosh* (1823) when Chief Justice John Marshall, in a case without any Native parties, dramatically modified historical understandings and suggested the doctrine of discovery **was a mechanism designed to prevent conflict between European competitors vying for lands in the New World**. However, he declared that in relations between colonizing powers and indigenous nations, the doctrine affirmed that tribal nations were the "rightful occupants of the soil," and acknowledged that they had "a legal as well as just claim to retain possession of it, and to use it according to their discretion."

While on the surface, Marshall's resurrection of the concept seems to support the case for indigenous property rights, the details of the decision were a major setback for Native peoples' sovereign territorial rights. **His interpretation gave the discovering state the exclusive or preemptive right to purchase land from the indigenous inhabitants. Even though Native nations had the right to own their lands, their right to sell was limited. In this sense, he wrote, "rights to complete sovereignty, as independent nations, were necessarily diminished**."

Birth rights and **nationality** were stolen by Christian European Nations.

Since then judicial rulings have referenced the doctrine. One of the most notable was *Tee-Hit-Ton v. United States* (1955) involving Alaskan Natives in which the Supreme Court equated the discovery doctrine with the doctrine of conquest. In that case, written during the Termination era, the discovery doctrine was misused to deny Alaskan Native nations any legal title to their lands, whatsoever. Justice Stanley F. Reed's inaccurate description of the Americans' alleged conquest of Natives bears repetition: "**Every American schoolboy knows that the savage tribes of this continent were deprived of their ancestral range by force and that, even when the Indians**

ceded millions of acres by treaty in return for blankets, food and trinkets, it was not a sale but the conquerors' will that deprived them of their land."

Reed's statement ranks among the most glaring and racist misrepresentations of fact ever uttered by a Supreme Court justice. Little in the historical record corroborates his contention that Alaskan Natives or many other Native peoples had been conquered, and, in fact, federal Indian policy and the history of treaty making give ample evidence to the contrary.

Nevertheless, this spurious decision has **never been overturned** and it **continues to undermine indigenous property rights**, as evidence by its citation in a recent 9th Circuit Court of Appeals decision, *White v. University of California* (August 2014), involving human remains of the Kumeyaay Nation of California.

To simplistically explain away loss of territory as the fault of the doctrine of discovery is to ignore our own retained land rights and forget that our ancestors were determined, intelligent, and politically astute people who defended their sovereign territories through strength and reason. To accept a dumbed-down version of history is to relegate our people to the role of victim. It is to accept that we have been conquered and as such are no more than rapidly disappearing ethnic groups of a by-gone era who no longer deserve the rights outlined in our treaties.

https://newsmaven.io/indiancountrytoday/archive/deconstructing-the-doctrine-of-discovery-vAHfau_vOkCfps7rRGPhAw/

The Flow of Sovereignty

In the United States, the Discovery Doctrine was enshrined in U.S. law by Supreme Court Justice John Marshall in 1823. In his landmark decision pertaining to indigenous land title, he explained that a European power gains radical title, or sovereignty, to any land it discovers. **Indigenous peoples who pre-date European or American sovereignty retain only the right of occupancy, which can still be dissolved by the federal government**.

When the United States gained independence from Britain, sovereignty flowed from Britain to the U.S. government. The flow of sovereignty excludes indigenous peoples, here in the United States and in lands around the world where the Doctrine of Discovery provides legal preference to Europeans. The Doctrine of Discovery was cited by the U.S. Supreme Court as the basis of our laws as recently as 2005. In the case *City of Sherrill, NY v. Oneida Nation*, justice Ruth Bader Ginsburg wrote the opinion on behalf of the court: "Under the 'doctrine of discovery' ... 'fee title [ownership] to the lands occupied by Indians when the colonists arrived became vested in the sovereign-first the discovering European nation and later the original states and the United States,'" quoting the 1974 case *Oneida Indian Nation of N.Y. v. County of Oneida*.

When Congress passed the National Defense Authorization Act of 2015, traditional ceremonial and burial sites sacred to the Apache People were sold to a foreign mining interest despite Apache protests that continued for more than a year. Senator John McCain ushered this defense spending bill through and included a rider handing off the land. The rider gave access to 2,400 acres of national forest land to Rio Tinto mine. As a national forest, this land was owned by the American People, and the Apache have been able to practice ceremony there. This land has enjoyed a special mining ban since 1955. With the passage of the Defense Authorization Act, it has become the private property of a foreign corporation, and a massive copper mine is planned.

Many people do not know that the apartheid system in South Africa was based on the reservation system in the United States and Canada. In 1910, the newly independent South Africa sent a delegation to Canada and the United States to observe how to develop a reservation system. They passed the Native Lands act in 1913, which ultimately left 87 percent of national lands for Whites only, with remaining 13 percent divided into "reserves."

Although South Africa's apartheid came to an end in 1994, our reservation system prevails. American Indian reservations do not enjoy representation in Congress. Indigenous tribes are considered "domestic dependent nations," and the Bureau of Indian Affairs, a federal agency, acts as guardian over indigenous peoples and their assets.

"**The Interior Department had failed to account for billions of dollars that they were supposed to collect on behalf of more than 300,000 Native Americans**," President Barack Obama stated upon the passing of Elouise Cobell, Niitsítapi elder and activist and lead plaintiff in the groundbreaking litigation *Cobell v. Salazar*, which challenged the Interior Department's mismanagement of funds.

Native Americans (**Blacks**, **colored**, **African-Americans, Negro**) are some of the most impoverished Americans. **This is because their wealth and assets were taken from them and given to members of another group**. This reality has not changed. Those who have reaped the economic benefit of the lands and resources of the United States have become wealthier over generations, **while Native Americans remain impoverished**.

Built In Bias

Using the logic of democracy, we equate "representation" with justice. But representation without institutional change only ensures that institutional power and levers are maneuvered by "diverse" people of power — the outcomes will be the same unless principles of equity are envisioned and embraced.

In the United States, **the wealth and influence wielded by those in power was taken from the first peoples of this land by force**. Those dispossessed are assumed to be represented according to the conventional wisdom of fairness. This fairness assumes we all have equal footing, we all begin from the same context. **When those with power assume this, indigenous peoples' experience**, **lived context**, **is denied**.

The church is called, as the Body of Christ, to seek to establish the kingdom of God. We cannot do this by collaborating with or by giving our consent to unjust and violent structures.

Our world is arranged by a system of institutions and laws. Slavery was an institution that was once pervasive in the world economy and enshrined in the laws of colonized countries. It did not fade away on its own — it had to be dismantled. Slavery came to an end when the laws that codified it and the policies of institutions that enforced it was dismantled. The same is true for apartheid and segregation. It was not easy to dismantle apartheid or segregation. But it was necessary. To affirm the human dignity of those oppressed by these structures, we must oppose the structures that are oppressive.
https://www.unitedmethodistwomen.org/news/the-ongoing-harm-of-the-doctrine-of-discovery

The injustices that Native peoples (**Blacks, African-American, colored, Negro**) face today are varied. Some, including **poverty**, **lack of access to quality health care and education**, **violence**

against women, **commodification of resources and environmental degradation**, affect many others in the United States, **but are exacerbated in Native communities because of jurisdictional issues and historic marginalization**. Other justice issues are unique to the lived experience of Native peoples. Many of those injustices flow from the Doctrine of Discovery and its legal and cultural successors, including the colonization and settlement of native lands, government policies that encouraged violence and forced assimilation, and the abrogation of sovereignty through broken treaties and court decisions.

Law

Beginning with the 1823 Johnson v. M'Intosh decision, the United States Supreme Court has used the Doctrine of Discovery as the basis for its decision making. The decision states, "**discovery gave an exclusive right to extinguish the Indian title of occupancy, either by purchase or by conquest**." **The United States owns Indigenous lands; the native people have only the legal right of** "**occupancy**." The decision, written by Chief Justice Marshall, further stated, "...**the tribes of Indians inhabiting this country were fierce savages, whose occupation was war, and whose subsistence was drawn chiefly from the forest. To leave them in possession of their country, was to leave the country a wilderness**." Unlike other racist court decisions from the nineteenth century, this decision has never been revisited or overturned. Later cases stated that **Indigenous peoples were domestic dependent nations of the United States**. The Johnson v. M'Intosh decision and those that followed continue to be cited in court cases and decisions today.

https://www.uua.org/multiculturalism/dod/effects-doctrine-discovery

Environment

In addition to the subjugation of indigenous peoples, the Doctrine of Discovery also had a devastating effect on the environment. The Discovery Doctrine **legally exiled those who had been stewards of their ecosystems for thousands of years and brought in people who had no knowledge of how to care for this land, and who based their economy and system on resource extraction**. During the Trail of Tears — the military order of President Andrew Jackson that displaced all Native American Nations in the Southeast to Oklahoma — **extremely valuable knowledge was lost to not only those Europeans in the Southeast about how to care for the land, but also to the newly settled Native American Nations**. As they were trying to adapt to new lands, many of them starved.

The European migrants stripped their new terrain of indigenous forests, fenced their property lines so their livestock would not wander, and **planted what they could, often without knowledge of the land**. They simply did all they could to set up a home like they had dreamed about in their home countries. With the support and blessing of laws, and a government in favor of their ownership, the new burgeoning country became a "rich country."

Today, after the rise of the U.S. as a world economic power, many of our global environmental concerns can be traced to this understanding of land ownership and an economic system based on resource extraction.

https://www.unitedmethodistwomen.org/news/the-enduring-effects-of-the-doctrine-of-discovery

Housing

The term refers to the presumed practice of mortgage lenders of drawing red lines around portions of a map to indicate areas or neighborhoods in which they do not want to make loans.

Redlining on a racial basis has been held by the courts to be an illegal practice. Google.com

Definition: *Redlining* is against the law, but that doesn't always stop violators. It is a discriminatory practice in real estate, typically involving lenders that refuse to lend money or extend credit to borrowers in certain areas of town or when realtors won't show properties to certain types of people in certain neighborhoods. **Those red-lined areas are typically occupied by people in poverty or people of color (Blacks, Negroes, African-American), or both**. It is against the law to discriminate against borrowers based on race or color, among other factors.

Redlining became known as such because lenders would literally draw a red line around a neighborhood on a map, often **targeting areas with a high concentration of people of color, and then refusing to lend in those areas because they considered the so-called "risk" too high**. Even though redlining is now against the law, major lenders today still end up in court over this despicable practice. You might rightfully wonder how is redlining still a thing? But then you would probably be a white person.

https://www.thebalance.com/definition-of-redlining-1798618

Housing values in American cities still break sharply along racial lines, showing the lingering impact of federal "redlining" in the **1930s, which devalued homes in African-American neighborhoods**. The practice was outlawed decades ago, but its effects are still evident. In fact, according to a study published last week by real estate website Zillow, the disparity has grown even worse over the past two decades.

More than 80 years ago, the government determined which neighborhoods it considered risky for federal mortgage loans, outlining the "riskiest" neighborhoods in red. The determining factor **was largely race**, regardless of the economic status of the residents.

By 1997, **homes in formerly redlined areas were worth less than half the value of homes in neighborhoods that had been deemed the "best" for mortgage lending**. Over the last two decades that gap has actually widened, according to analysis of home values across the nation.

Median home prices in the communities across the country deemed "best" in the 1930s were about $640,000, or close to two-and-one-half times more than those in redlined communities, where national median price was $276,000 as of 2017.

That gap, according to one housing analyst, shows the nagging legacy of segregation and racist housing policies playing itself out in the modern housing market, despite legislative reforms and booming urban housing markets.

"It's a **legacy of segregation** and the effect of that legacy on intergenerational poverty," says Gustavo Velasquez, director of the Urban Institute's Washington-Area Research Initiative and a former assistant secretary for fair housing and equal opportunity at HUD under President Obama. "It takes a long time to overcome what happened 80 years ago."

In 1934, the federal government began issuing mortgages through the Home Owners' Loan Corporation. The agency created maps showing where mortgages were the riskiest and areas where those loans were deemed safe bets. **Race, not economic well-being, was the deciding factor**. "A neighborhood earned a red color if African Americans lived in it, even if it was a solid middle-class neighborhood of single-family homes," Richard Rothstein wrote in *The Color of Law: A Forgotten History of How Our Government Segregated America*.

Small businesses and large developers alike steered money to other areas during this period, contributing to the blight of black neighborhoods over the next several decades. Redlining was finally banned in 1968 under the Fair Housing Act.

Even in today's hottest real estate markets, including Brooklyn and the San Francisco Bay Area, homes in neighborhoods that were labelled the most desirable in the 1930s are still at least twice as valuable today. In Chicago, those homes are almost three times as valuable now.
https://www.governing.com/topics/transportation-infrastructure/gov-redlining-race-real-estate-values-lc.html

Insurance

Redlining a discriminatory practice by which banks, insurance companies, etc., refuse or limit loans, mortgages, insurance, etc., within specific geographic areas, **especially inner-city neighborhoods**. Google.com

An underwriting practice involving the rejection of a risk based solely on geographical location. This practice is prohibited under the laws of most states as it tends to be **discriminatory to minorities**. https://www.irmi.com/term/insurance-definitions/redlining

Redlining is an unethical practice that puts services (financial and otherwise) out of reach for residents of certain areas based on race or ethnicity. It can be seen in the systematic denial of mortgages, insurance, loans and other financial services based on location (and that area's default history) rather than an individual's qualifications and creditworthiness. Notably, the policy of **redlining is felt the most by residents of minority neighborhoods**.

The term "redlining" was coined by sociologist James McKnight in the 1960s based on how lenders would literally draw a red line on a map around the neighborhoods they would not invest in based on demographics alone. **Black (Aboriginal Americans), inner city neighborhoods were most likely to be redlined**. **Investigations found that lenders would make loans to lower-income whites but not to middle- or upper-income African Americans**. Examples of redlining can be found in a variety of financial services, including mortgages, student loans, credit cards and insurance.

https://www.investopedia.com/terms/r/redlining.asp

Banking

Redlining is an unethical practice that puts services (financial and otherwise) out of reach for residents of certain areas based on race or ethnicity. Google.com

Fifty years after the federal Fair Housing Act banned racial discrimination in lending, **African Americans and Latinos continue to be routinely denied conventional mortgage loans at rates far higher than their white counterparts**.

This modern-day redlining persisted in 61 metro areas even when controlling for applicants' income, loan amount and neighborhood, according to millions of Home Mortgage Disclosure Act records analyzed by Reveal from The Center for Investigative Reporting.

The yearlong analysis, based on 31 million records, relied on techniques used by leading academics, the Federal Reserve and Department of Justice to identify lending disparities.

It found a pattern of troubling denials for people of color across the country, including in major metropolitan areas such as Atlanta, Detroit, Philadelphia, Rockford, Ill., St. Louis and San Antonio.

African Americans faced the most resistance in Southern cities - Mobile, Alabama; Greenville, North Carolina; and Gainesville, Florida - and Latinos in Iowa City, Iowa.

No matter their location, loan applicants told similar stories, describing an uphill battle with loan officers who they said seemed to be fishing for a reason to say no.

In the 1930s, surveyors with the federal Home Owners' Loan Corporation drew lines on maps and colored some neighborhoods red, deeming them "hazardous" for bank lending because of the presence of African Americans or European immigrants, especially Jews.

Redlining has been outlawed for half a century. And for the last 40 years, banks have had a legal obligation under the Community Reinvestment Act to solicit clients - borrowers and depositors - from all segments of their communities.

But in many places, Reveal found **the law hasn't made much difference**.

The analysis - independently reviewed and confirmed by The Associated Press - showed black applicants were turned away at significantly higher rates than whites in 48 cities, Latinos in 25, Asians in nine and Native Americans in three. In Washington, D.C., the nation's capital, Reveal found all four groups were significantly more likely to be denied a home loan than whites.

The disproportionate denials and limited anti-discrimination enforcement help explain why the homeownership gap between whites and African Americans is now wider than it was during the Jim Crow era.

In the United States, "wealth and financial stability are inextricably linked to housing opportunity and homeownership," said Lisa

Rice, executive vice president of the National Fair Housing Alliance, an advocacy group. "For a typical family, the largest share of their wealth emanates from homeownership and home equity."

The latest figures from the U.S. Census Bureau show the median net worth for an African American family is now $9,000, compared with $132,000 for a white family. Latino families did not fare much better at $12,000.

http://www.chicagotribune.com/business/ct-biz-modern-day-redlining-20180215-story.html

Education

Redlining was the once-common practice in which banks would draw a red line on a map—often along a natural barrier like a highway or river—to designate neighborhoods where they would not invest. Stigmatized and denied access to loans and other resources, redlined communities, populated by **African-Americans and other people of color, often became places that lacked businesses, jobs, grocery stores and other services, and thus could not retain a thriving middle class**. **Redlining produced and reinforced a vicious cycle of decline for which residents themselves were typically blamed**.

https://www.thenation.com/article/why-congress-redlining-our-schools/

While growing up, lower income students may have less access to educational books and magazines in the home, educational computer programs, and the cultural capital known to have a positive effect on academic achievement such as trips to museums and theaters (Conley and Yeung, 2008). Lower income students are more likely to have a job to alleviate the financial burden on their families which gives them less time to focus on school work. They are also more likely to not have access to internet and computers at home which further makes it harder for them to complete their homework. Their parents are more likely to work more jobs or odd shifts which gives them less time to help their children with their studies or to be able to constantly focus on encouraging them to do their best in academics. If the student is having trouble in their studies, their parents also may not be able to afford a tutor to assist them.

http://modernsegregationineducation.web.unc.edu/sample-page-2/

The aforementioned high-poverty communities result from the disparities created by residential segregation by lowering the price of property and tax returns. Even after the passing of the Civil Rights Act of 1964 and Fair Housing Act of 1968, residential segregation has continued to exist. This allows for racial stereotypes to be perpetuated and can lead to social isolation for inner-city inhabitants in and out of the school. **This is important because elevated levels of segregation broaden racial disparity and limit the economic performance of major cities by allowing areas of poverty to bloom. Even most residents of inner-city communities are unwilling to stay when given the opportunity**. Low property values as a result of residential segregation means that people would rather leave than stay behind and spur residential development. (Gamoran 2007; Sharpe 2009)

Low property values have a negative effect on inner-city schools because of the way primary and secondary schools are funded. Schools rely heavily on state taxes and local property revenue/taxes, which are based on accessed property values. Accessed property values are higher for people with higher socioeconomic status. What this means is that individuals living in richer neighborhoods pay more taxes. Therefore, they are able afford better quality educators and overall better quality school facilities. **However, 'redlining' contributed to economic decline in urban areas by forcing businesses to relocate to more prosperous areas**. As a result, the inner-city has much lower property values and people of low socioeconomic status (SES) cannot afford to pay higher taxes. **Because inner-city students cannot afford the quality of education available to middle and upper class families they are forced to learn in underfunded and understaffed schools**. (Vernez, Kropp, and Rydell 1999) Redlining, the Roots of Educational Inequality by Jovan Radicevic

Employment

While many black people are intimately familiar with the practice of redlining (which refers to a combination of housing discrimination and obstructive lending practices which prevent blacks from obtaining home ownership), **it is difficult for others to concede the idea that wealth has been systematically denied from blacks long after segregation ended**. Recent economic research not only continues to confirm the existence of redlining but also shows **that redlining never went away**—and is part of the reason that the wealth gap between whites and blacks remains so stark to this day.

Though there a number of factors which could contribute to the differences in mobility, **redlining, as well as employment discrimination, are two key practices that economists are studying in order to understand the long-term economic harm done to blacks in America**. **(Aboriginal Americans) The bottom line is that by forcing blacks into certain neighborhoods, restricting them from loans that allowed them to buy homes, and well forcing them into lower-paying jobs, they do not have the same opportunities**

to create wealth as whites and this is, in part, why inequality still remains.

Though so much of this kind of systemic inequality is proven by facts and research, invariably conversations about race and economics will still end up devolving into the bootstrap myth and pathological stereotypes of black people. Some folks will still say that black people are at fault themselves for the wealth gap and have been given every opportunity since 1964 and the passage of the Civil Rights Act to catch up to whites. Such perspectives are not only ahistorical, they reflect a lack of critical understanding about the ways in which generational wealth is transferred—an important vehicle for moving wealth from generation to generation. **Currently, the average black family would need 228 years to build the wealth of a white family today.**

"A family with some assets can help their kids pay for an education or put a down payment on a first home or kick them some seed money to start a small business. All of those things help the next generation climb the economic ladder." [...]

According to Princeton University sociologist Dalton Conley, **the wealth of a child's family is the single greatest predictor of that child's future economic prospects**. Conley, whose data did include things like cars and household goods, found that even white households hovering around the poverty line have a net worth of $10,000 to $15,000, but the typical black family at that income level will often be under water, with a negative net worth.

https://www.dailykos.com/stories/2017/7/21/1682804/-Persistent-redlining-and-employment-discrimination-have-hurt-black-Americans-chance-at-wealth

Mass Incarceration, Stress, and Aboriginal American Infant Mortality

Infant mortality and mass incarceration are major issues affecting the black community. **(Aboriginal Americans)** But while they are often thought of and dealt with on separate tracks, structural racism firmly connects these critical issues. **Structural racism exposes black women to distinct stressors**—such as contact with the criminal justice system—that ultimately undermine their health and the health of their children. Today, **infants born to black mothers die at twice the rate as those born to white mothers**. This horrific disparity cannot be fully explained by differences in income, education, or even health care; **evidence suggests that cumulative stress from generations of structural racism is driving this epidemic**. To combat this persistent problem, lawmakers must attack structural racism in all its forms—including mass incarceration.

On a side note in regards to stress from generations of structural racism:

Dr. Rachel Yehuda, professor of psychiatry at Icahn School of Medicine at Mount Sinai, has conducted a depth of research into epigenetics and the intergenerational transmission of trauma. In layman's terms, she is researching how serious incidents of trauma (i.e. slavery, holocaust, etc.) and post-traumatic stress disorder (PTSD) can be passed down through generations in shared family genes. Her research has revealed that when people experience trauma, it changes their genes in a very specific and noticeable way, so when those people have children and their genes are passed down to their children, **the children also inherit the genes affected by trauma**.

https://www.teenvogue.com/story/slavery-trauma-inherited-genetics

Structural racism is defined as a system of public policies, institutional practices, cultural representations, and other norms that work in reinforcing ways to perpetuate racial inequality. The criminal justice system is perhaps the clearest example of structural racism in the United States. The United States has the highest incarceration rate in the world, and the overwhelming burden of contact with the system has fallen on communities of color, especially African Americans. **African American adults are five times more likely to be imprisoned than white Americans**. According to data detailed in this issue brief**, African Americans are twice as likely as their white counterparts to have a family member imprisoned at some point during their childhood**. With overall incarceration rates more than 500 percent higher than they were forty years ago, black Millennials and post-Millennials are at greater risk of contact with the system than any previous generation. In fact, a new CAP analysis finds that 1 in 4 black Millennials had an incarcerated loved one before they even turned 18. For those born in the early 1990s, the rate is almost 1 in 3.

Mass incarceration has long-term physiological effects that contribute to a range of health issues, including mental health disorders, diabetes, asthma, hypertension, HIV, and Hepatitis C. Although not as well-studied, mass incarceration can also directly and indirectly affect infant mortality. While its direct effects are well-documented, its indirect effects are pervasive and damaging but largely unrecognized. When incarcerated, an individual can face increased risk of sexual violence and infectious illness; loss of connection with family and friends; as well as trauma resulting from draconian prison policies and practices. Furthermore, the incarceration of a loved one or breadwinner can cause families and friends significant emotional distress, loss of income and property, and residential instability. **These experiences put affected individuals at a heightened**

risk of post-traumatic stress disorder (PTSD), anxiety, and depression.

Based off new analysis and existing evidence, the Center for American Progress believes **the toxic stress from contact with the criminal justice system has contributed to the disparity in rates of black and white infant mortality**. In fact, experts estimate that infant mortality rates today would be 7.8 percent lower and that disparities between black and white women would be 15 percent smaller if incarceration rates had remained at 1970s levels. Targeted interventions are necessary to close the gap and bring the United States up to par with other developed countries.

This issue brief presents a new CAP analysis and summarizes existing research to detail the effects of mass incarceration on black women and children. In particular, it highlights how black women's heightened contact with the criminal justice system leads to increased stress and disparities in health and infant mortality.

Structural racism exposes countless black women and children to the harmful stressors associated with the criminal justice system. The number of incarcerated U.S. women overall has increased dramatically in recent decades—from just 26,000 in 1980 to 219,000 in 2017. Perhaps unsurprisingly, the spike in female incarceration has disproportionately affected black women, especially young black women. While black women overall are twice as likely to be imprisoned as their white counterparts, black women ages 18 to 19 are three times more likely to be imprisoned than their white counterparts. If current incarceration trends continue, 1 in 18 black women will be imprisoned at some point in their lifetime.

Black women and their families, especially within younger generations, are also more likely than their white counterparts to have indirect contact with the criminal justice system through the incarceration of a household member. According to new CAP analysis of data from nine states, African American children across generations have had more than twice the odds of having an incarcerated household member as white children. This is true even after controlling for income level; geography; and family history of addiction, mental illness, and abuse. The data also reveal that younger generations are at greater risk, with 27.4 percent of black Millennials having indirect contact during childhood, compared with 10.7 percent of black Baby Boomers.

Millions of black women are exposed to the harmful effects of mass incarceration during their lifetimes. Whether they experience imprisonment personally or they have an incarcerated loved one, contact with the system is a significant stressor that undermines the long-term health of mothers and their children.

Furthermore, the vast majority of incarcerated women are also mothers—mostly to young children. Prior to incarceration, most of these women were the primary caretakers of their children. But half are confined in facilities located more than 100 miles from their families, and more than one-third (38 percent) will not see their children even once while incarcerated. Lack of regular contact with their children heightens stress levels among incarcerated mothers. To make matters worse, many siblings are split up when a mother is imprisoned. When this occurs, incarcerated mothers are four times more likely to experience high levels of maternal strain—or significant stress from feeling like they are not fulfilling their obligations as a mother. In addition, if children are placed in foster care, incarcerated mothers risk never getting them back, even if they are able to demonstrate the ability to care for them upon release. Black mothers are already far more likely to report depression than the general population. These stressors only exacerbate this persistent problem.

These traumatic experiences produce mental and physical scars that undermine the long-term health and well-being of women and their infants. As discussed above, black women are overrepresented in the criminal justice system and thus at heightened risk of exposure to these unique stressors. This reality contributes to health disparities between African American women and white women.

Infants born to black mothers are dying at high rates. According to the Centers for Disease Control and Prevention (CDC), they are more than twice as likely to die as infants born to white mothers. In seeking to explain this disparity, researchers have discovered that protective factors such as education, income, and health care reduce infant mortality rates for many women but do not necessarily reduce the risks for black women.

Achieving postsecondary education, for example, decreases the risk of infant mortality for white women by 20 percent. For black women, however, **the same accomplishment has no effect on risk of infant mortality**. And while increasing income in adulthood decreases the risk of infant mortality for white women who experienced childhood poverty by 50 percent, the same experience did not have a statistically significant effect for black women. The National Institutes of Health recommend early and regular prenatal care to improve chances of a healthy pregnancy. But black women who receive early and regular prenatal care are still at greater risk of infant mortality than white women who receive no prenatal care. While well-known protective factors may help some women, the evidence is clear—a different type of intervention is needed to help black women and their infants.

An emerging body of research suggests that cumulative stress from enduring a lifetime of structural racism is undermining black women's health and creating disparities in infant and maternal mortality. Efforts to measure the physiological effects of long-term stress have found that black women are twice as likely as their white counterparts to exhibit high levels of stress. The "weathering hypothesis" offers insight into the high levels of stress black women experience. This hypothesis and subsequent research suggest that enduring racism over a lifetime increases stress and ultimately undermines the health of black mothers and their infants. A previous CAP analysis found that black women are five times more likely than white women to report adverse physical and emotional symptoms because of recent race-based societal discrimination.

https://www.americanprogress.org/issues/race/reports/2018/06/05/451647/mass-incarceration-stress-black-infant-mortality/

A Few More Things

The Doctrine of Discovery shapes current reality for indigenous peoples. I would argue **there are no instances in which land rights have been restored** or the impact of the Doctrine of Discovery lost to time.

The Doctrine of Discovery, and the power it has wielded in **shaping our society**, **determines who shapes our institutions**. **It defines how we define justice**. It is not unusual in our culture to define justice in terms of "fairness" rather than equity. Fairness is often described in the terms of the powerful, without context. Fairness for the powerful is defined as equal distribution of a good without acknowledgement of unequal standing. According to conventional wisdom about fairness, the majority has a right to the majority of resources and therefore has a right to the most power.

https://dofdmenno.org/2016/10/26/the-ongoing-harm-of-the-doctrine-of-discovery/

"... most people are simply unaware that this blatantly racist European colonial era legal doctrine continues to be **used by courts and policy makers in the West's most advanced Nation states to deny indigenous peoples (so-called Blacks, African-Americans, Negroes) their basic human rights guaranteed under principles of modern international law**. The contemporary global movement for indigenous peoples' human rights is a direct response to the anxieties and distress caused by these types of dehumanizing legal principles adhered to by "civilized" states around the world today."

~ Robert A. Williams, Jr., *Savage Anxieties: The Invention of Western Civilization* (New

York: Palgrave Macmillan, 2012), at 228.

The consequences of the past wrongs regarding the taking of Indigenous lands and resources are visible worldwide, through **debilitating impoverishment and suffering endured by Indigenous peoples**. In Canada, the Royal Commission on Aboriginal
Peoples concluded in its 1996 Report: "Without adequate lands and resources, Aboriginal nations ... will be *pushed to the edge of economic, cultural and political extinction*."

https://www.fgcquaker.org/sites/default/files/attachments/Resources%20on%20the%20Doctrine%20of%20Discovery%20from%20Canadian%20Friends%20Service%20Committee.pdf

The doctrine's modern influence re-emerged recently in the debate about the racism and exploitation of Native American **sports mascots**, Fiedler said. It has justified efforts to eliminate indigenous languages, practices and worldviews, and it affects Native American sovereignty and treaty obligations.

https://www.globalsistersreport.org/equality/nuns-pope-revoke-15th-century-doctrine-allows-christians-seize-native-land-10636

Discovery is a strange, even bizarre, piece of the American legal code but one that has been incredibly complex and **a vitally important legal tool for Euro-Christian colonization**, particularly in North America. As such, **it has been critically important to the Lutheran occupation of American land. It snatched Minnesota away from Native Peoples**, for example, and secured it as largely Lutheran and catholic properties, using legal and theological language to justify thievery as righteous Christian acts. Indeed, **Discovery is yet today the legal and theological foundation for private ownership of all real estate property in the U.S**. We should add that Discovery is also a **fiction, a legal invention; yet it has succeeded wildly in its intended aim**.

At the outset, then, we need to understand that the Doctrine is **explicitly theological and Christian legal discourse**, firmly predicated on a global pronouncement made by a catholic pope more than two decades before the Lutheran reformation. Nevertheless, **it was also the legal principle used by every protestant Christian group who made claims to Native land in North America**, **from the Episcopalians at Jamestown to the Puritans and pilgrims in New England—and Lutheran immigrants who swept across the northern tier of the U.S. claiming Indian land as their own properties**. Readers of this journal may argue that Discovery is certainly not Lutheran theology, but for all practical purposes that is irrelevant. **Anyone who owns a home in America, or for that matter rents a home, is a full participant (wittingly or not) in the theology of Christian Discovery even as they live by the laws that have ensued**.

By the 1750s a young George Washington was functioning on the basis of a clear understanding of the Doctrine of Discovery—as a **surveyor taking care to nail down the best Indian lands in the Ohio valley as personal investments and for the Washington family land business**. It was still Indian country inhabited by and controlled by Seneca's and numerous other communities of the Ohio League. It took an all-out war of destruction, declared by Washington as commander of the continental army and then continuing under his presidency, to wrest the land away from the Ohio League and allow Christian settlers to cash in on Washington's investments. A decade after Washington's tour in the Ohio Valley, in the 1760s and 70s, **Thomas Jefferson began his legal career, gaining considerable renown using the principle of Discovery in legal cases involving property rights in Virginia**. Then in 1803, as president, Jefferson clearly exercised Discovery in the so-called Louisiana Purchase. Twenty years later, John Marshall wrote his famous unanimous decision in the Johnson v. M'Intosh Supreme Court case, deciding American property ownership on the basis of Christian Discovery. We turn to Jefferson and Marshall for two key pieces of the puzzle.

So, in 1803, the United States bought my land, Osage land (now mostly the modern state of Missouri)—**from France**! Jefferson did not, however, buy any actual "property," which undoubtedly comes as a big surprise to most high school history students. **No, the U.S. only bought the Euro-Christian legal pre-emptory right of Christian) Discovery, the only thing France had to sell**. This was not insignificant. Even if the U.S. could not (yet) claim actual ownership of property, **it did portend the extension of U.S. sovereignty and the eventual (and not too distant) conversion of the entire territory to "real property," that is, legally designated property, so defined by the Euro-Christian Rule of Law**. **To ensure U.S. possession of the entire territory, Jefferson proceeded to send a military unit, the**

Corps of Discovery (i.e., Lewis and Clark), to enact the legal rituals of Discovery to seal the deal. Needless to say, the whole transaction transpired without U.S. politicians' contemplation **of negotiating the acquisition with any of the current occupants**, that is, **the several dozen sovereign Native nations that lived on their lands, now suddenly U.S. territory**. This is the Euro-Christian Rule of Law, deeply rooted in a theology of Christian identity.

This Louisiana Purchase was just the beginning. **Converting Indian land into the Euro-Christian category of "property" would involve a longer legal/military process of Euro-Christian deceit and force. Jefferson ensured the second part of the Discovery process would begin almost immediately, using language to achieve the goal by carefully naming the Lewis and Clark expedition in terms of Discovery**. This was not mere courageous romance and adventure, or the exciting expansion of the American frontier. Rather, **it established an ironclad Christian legal claim to other peoples' homes**!

Thus like Spain in California three decades earlier, Jefferson was sending a military unit to perform the historically defined acts and rituals associated with Discovery – to mark the territory as the legal expansion of American sovereignty over the territory of Louisiana west of the Mississippi – and even to extend the American claim to that territory of the pacific northwest that was as yet unclaimed by any other Christian nation.] Of course, Native nations already lived across the entire expanse. Thus, **one important aspect of Lewis and Clark's charge was to announce to Indians that the United States was the new sovereign of the whole immense territory**. Ultimately, their rituals of Discovery were intended to reify American possession.

[13] To grasp Jefferson's explicit understanding of the Doctrine of Discovery in appointing this expedition, one has to wait for an

Indian historian and legal scholar to do the extensive archival research necessary. Shawnee scholar, Robert Miller, demonstrates from countless Jeffersonian documents that **Jefferson was perfectly clear that his expedition was formally exercising Discovery on behalf of the United States As a real estate lawyer and a land dealer himself**, **Jefferson ascended the presidency with a firm grasp and practiced understanding of the Discovery principles**. He never uses the word Discovery in any formal legal context—until naming the Lewis and Clark expedition, **yet it is clear that he did indeed function both legally and politically with a clear understanding of the foundational Euro-Christian law**. The importance of Jefferson's knowledge becomes apparent in the sheer mass of legal cases (over 400) he handled involving land and land title.

In the context of religious disestablishment and the separation of church and state, the blessing of a church was no longer deemed necessary for enacting (Christian) Discovery, unlike the Spanish Discovery act in California in which Gaspar de Portola was partnered with (now) St. Junípero to accomplish the religious side of Discovery (1770). Still, there were legal trappings that had to be observed and performed, both to ensure the United States' right of Discovery to the Louisiana territory **and to extend those claims further to the northwest**. Miller demonstrates that **Lewis and Clark "engaged in an amalgamation" of the formal and legal Discovery rituals that had been practiced by Euro-Christian nations of Europe since Columbus as they competed with one another to claim as much foreign property as each could – and give their land grabbing some legal clothing. It is abundantly apparent that Lewis and Clark were exercising great care, Miller reports, "to ensure that they used all the rituals necessary to make Discovery claims."**

Just as clearly as the Spanish duo on the beach at Monterey in 1770, **Lewis and Clark were enacting the rituals of Discovery to ensure that their "Christian prince," the invasive sovereign called the United States, could legally and morally claim ownership of someone else's land**. The expedition, concludes Miller, is a living embodiment of Discovery. Like Portola and Serra and countless other Euro-Christian adventurers, they "took physical possession of land, built permanent structures, engaged in parades and formal procedures of possession and occupation, tried to obtain native consent to American possession, and engaged in mapmaking and celestial observations." **Lewis even wrote a 2500-word speech that was recited to each Native nation they encountered—in English! The speech explained to Indian folk the new, Discovery-based political structure of American sovereignty. Native leaders were given gifts of medals and American flags, marking those people as well as their territory as belonging now to the U.S.**

At the same time, **Lewis was careful to delineate the new relationship of parent and child to the Native community**. From that time on, **the president of the United States – again, only in English– was to be known as the Great Father. Indians were to be his "children" – and should therefore be obedient children, not unlike the expectation of St. Junípero for Indians locked in his missions**. In their typical romanticized interpretations of the Lewis and Clark expedition, historians like Albert Furtwangler or Stephen Ambrose overlook these explicit legal discourses embedded in the actions of the Corps of Discovery. It is all merely a part of the American romance of continental conquest and American exceptionalism. For the Osage People, Lewis and Clark is a tragic narrative describing how we lost our land, all done legally, with perfect attention to the (Christian) Rule of Law—however artificial and made up it might have been.

https://www.elca.org/JLE/Articles/1203

Wars

Another root of the Doctrine of Discovery lie in the Crusades, a long series of religious wars spanning a period of 600 years (1095 to 1699) that have left a deep mark on western thinking. When Pope Urban II launched the first Crusade to compel Christians to conquer Jerusalem, a land settled and ruled by Muslims for centuries, his imperial battle cry was "God wills this!" (Deus hoc vult!).[11] As Christians remodeled a theological edifice built on Jewish foundations, they adapted the concept of the Chosen People for themselves and claimed the Promised Land to be anywhere they settled, providing a convenient justification for the conquest and enslavement of other peoples.

By the end of the Middle Ages the word "crusade" had come to refer to all wars undertaken on God's behalf. Crusading – God commanding Christians to wage pre-emptive war – became a controlling idea. **Because people must be evil (controlled by the Devil) to oppose the will of God, the non-Christian enemy was always deemed intractable and had to be exterminated for the safety of the community**. **Any people judged barbarian, not living by civilized (i.e. Christian) standards, were subject to colonization for the same reasons. The white Christian man's burden was to colonize in order to save every human being in the world**.

The Conquistadores, who went forth to discover "new" (non Christian-ruled) lands considered themselves to be soldiers of the cross on holy crusades. Vasco da Gama, Christopher Columbus and Hernan Cortez all wore the cross on their breast, on their sails and, besides their commercial goals, hoped to attack Islamic rulers from the rear by circumnavigating Africa or reaching Asia. The popes strongly encouraged these expeditions.

The Spanish, including Columbus, did not use the word conquer, much less invade. **All pronouncements and laws issued by the throne used discover and pacify, even when referring to armed intervention**.

Religious repression was even harsher for those indigenous peoples who were able to organize serious resistance. Idols were destroyed, temples burned and those who celebrated Native rites were punished by death; festivities such as banquets, songs and dances, as well as artistic and intellectual activities (painting, sculpture, observations of stars, hieroglyphic writing) – all suspected of being inspired by the devil – were forbidden, and those who took part in them mercilessly hunted down and enslaved or murdered.

Through this long, violent period of consolidation of control over much of Europe, Africa and the Americas, the rationale for conquest slowly secularized. At first, people were attacked because they were not Christian. Then, they were attacked because they were not reasonable, because any reasonable person would be a Christian. Finally, they were attacked because they were not civilized, because any civilized society would embrace Christianity and Christians' attempt to civilize them.

Protestants colonizers were no different than Catholic ones. For example, the Puritan patent (charter) for land from the Massachusetts Bay Company stated explicitly:

The principall Ende of this Plantacion is to Wynn and incite the natives of [the] country, to the Knowledge and Obedience of the onlie true God and Savior of Mankind, and the Christian Fayth.

Legislation passed in 1644 outlawed the practice of Native religion and committed the entire colony to the missionary effort.

https://christianhegemony.org/the-doctrine-of-discovery-manifest-destiny-and-american-exceptionalism

Year-by-year Timeline of America's Major Wars (1776-2011)

1776 – American Revolutionary War, Chickamagua Wars, Second Cherokee War, Pennamite-Yankee War

1777 – American Revolutionary War, Chickamauga Wars, Second Cherokee War, Pennamite-Yankee War

1778 – American Revolutionary War, Chickamauga Wars, Pennamite-Yankee War

1779 – American Revolutionary War, Chickamauga Wars, Pennamite-Yankee War

1780 – American Revolutionary War, Chickamauga Wars, Pennamite-Yankee War

1781 – American Revolutionary War, Chickamauga Wars, Pennamite-Yankee War

1782 – American Revolutionary War, Chickamauga Wars, Pennamite-Yankee War

1783 – American Revolutionary War, Chickamauga Wars, Pennamite-Yankee War

1784 – Chickamauga Wars, Pennamite-Yankee War, Oconee War

1785 – Chickamauga Wars, Northwest Indian War

1786 – Chickamauga Wars, Northwest Indian War

1787 – Chickamauga Wars, Northwest Indian War

1788 – Chickamauga Wars, Northwest Indian War

1789 – Chickamauga Wars, Northwest Indian War

1790 – Chickamauga Wars, Northwest Indian War

1791 – Chickamauga Wars, Northwest Indian War

1792 – Chickamauga Wars, Northwest Indian War

1793 – Chickamauga Wars, Northwest Indian War

1794 – Chickamauga Wars, Northwest Indian War

1795 – Northwest Indian War

1796 – No major war

1797 – No major war

1798 – Quasi-War

1799 – Quasi-War

1800 – Quasi-War

1801 – First Barbary War

1802 – First Barbary War

1803 – First Barbary War

1804 – First Barbary War

1805 – First Barbary War

1806 – Sabine Expedition

1807 – No major war

1808 – No major war

1809 – No major war

1810 – U.S. occupies Spanish-held West Florida

1811 – Tecumseh's War

1812 – War of 1812, Tecumseh's War, Seminole Wars, U.S. occupies Spanish-held Amelia Island and other parts of East Florida

1813 – War of 1812, Tecumseh's War, Peoria War, Creek War, U.S. expands its territory in West Florida

1814 – War of 1812, Creek War, U.S. expands its territory in Florida, Anti-piracy war

1815 – War of 1812, Second Barbary War, Anti-piracy war

1816 – First Seminole War, Anti-piracy war

1817 – First Seminole War, Anti-piracy war

1818 – First Seminole War, Anti-piracy war

1819 – Yellowstone Expedition, Anti-piracy war

1820 – Yellowstone Expedition, Anti-piracy war

1821 – Anti-piracy war (see note above)

1822 – Anti-piracy war (see note above)

1823 – Anti-piracy war, Arikara War

1824 – Anti-piracy war

1825 – Yellowstone Expedition, Anti-piracy war

1826 – No major war

1827 – Winnebago War

1828 – No major war

1829 – No major war

1830 – No major war

1831 – Sac and Fox Indian War

1832 – Black Hawk War

1833 – Cherokee Indian War

1834 – Cherokee Indian War, Pawnee Indian Territory Campaign

1835 – Cherokee Indian War, Seminole Wars, Second Creek War

1836 – Cherokee Indian War, Seminole Wars, Second Creek War, Missouri-Iowa Border War

1837 – Cherokee Indian War, Seminole Wars, Second Creek War, Osage Indian War, Buckshot War

1838 – Cherokee Indian War, Seminole Wars, Buckshot War, Heatherly Indian War

1839 – Cherokee Indian War, Seminole Wars

1840 – Seminole Wars, U.S. naval forces invade Fiji Islands

1841 – Seminole Wars, U.S. naval forces invade McKean Island, Gilbert Islands, and Samoa

1842 – Seminole Wars

1843 – U.S. forces clash with Chinese, U.S. troops invade African coast

1844 – Texas-Indian Wars

1845 – Texas-Indian Wars

1846 – Mexican-American War, Texas-Indian Wars

1847 – Mexican-American War, Texas-Indian Wars

1848 – Mexican-American War, Texas-Indian Wars, Cayuse War

1849 – Texas-Indian Wars, Cayuse War, Southwest Indian Wars, Navajo Wars, Skirmish between 1st Cavalry and Indians

1850 – Texas-Indian Wars, Cayuse War, Southwest Indian Wars, Navajo Wars, Yuma War, California Indian Wars, Pitt River Expedition

1851 – Texas-Indian Wars, Cayuse War, Southwest Indian Wars, Navajo Wars, Apache Wars, Yuma War, Utah Indian Wars, California Indian Wars

1852 – Texas-Indian Wars, Cayuse War, Southwest Indian Wars, Navajo Wars, Yuma War, Utah Indian Wars, California Indian Wars

1853 – Texas-Indian Wars, Cayuse War, Southwest Indian Wars, Navajo Wars, Yuma War, Utah Indian Wars, Walker War, California Indian Wars

1854 – Texas-Indian Wars, Cayuse War, Southwest Indian Wars, Navajo Wars, Apache Wars, California Indian Wars, Skirmish between 1st Cavalry and Indians

1855 – Seminole Wars, Texas-Indian Wars, Cayuse War, Southwest Indian Wars, Navajo Wars, Apache Wars, California

Indian Wars, Yakima War, Winnas Expedition, Klickitat War, Puget Sound War, Rogue River Wars, U.S. forces invade Fiji Islands and Uruguay

1856 – Seminole Wars, Texas-Indian Wars, Southwest Indian Wars, Navajo Wars, California Indian Wars, Puget Sound War, Rogue River Wars, Tintic War

1857 – Seminole Wars, Texas-Indian Wars, Southwest Indian Wars, Navajo Wars, California Indian Wars, Utah War, Conflict in Nicaragua

1858 – Seminole Wars, Texas-Indian Wars, Southwest Indian Wars, Navajo Wars, Mohave War, California Indian Wars, Spokane-Coeur d'Alene-Paloos War, Utah War, U.S. forces invade Fiji Islands and Uruguay

1859 Texas-Indian Wars, Southwest Indian Wars, Navajo Wars, California Indian Wars, Pecos Expedition, Antelope Hills Expedition, Bear River Expedition, John Brown's raid, U.S. forces launch attack against Paraguay, U.S. forces invade Mexico

1860 – Texas-Indian Wars, Southwest Indian Wars, Navajo Wars, Apache Wars, California Indian Wars, Paiute War, Kiowa-Comanche War

1861 – American Civil War, Texas-Indian Wars, Southwest Indian Wars, Navajo Wars, Apache Wars, California Indian Wars, Cheyenne Campaign

1862 – American Civil War, Texas-Indian Wars, Southwest Indian Wars, Navajo Wars, Apache Wars, California Indian Wars, Cheyenne Campaign, Dakota War of 1862,

1863 – American Civil War, Texas-Indian Wars, Southwest Indian Wars, Navajo Wars, Apache Wars, California Indian Wars, Cheyenne Campaign, Colorado War, Goshute War

1864 – American Civil War, Texas-Indian Wars, Navajo Wars, Apache Wars, California Indian Wars, Cheyenne Campaign, Colorado War, Snake War

1865 – American Civil War, Texas-Indian Wars, Navajo Wars, Apache Wars, California Indian Wars, Colorado War, Snake War, Utah's Black Hawk War

1866 – Texas-Indian Wars, Navajo Wars, Apache Wars, California Indian Wars, Skirmish between 1st Cavalry and Indians, Snake War, Utah's Black Hawk War, Red Cloud's War, Franklin County War, U.S. invades Mexico, Conflict with China

1867 – Texas-Indian Wars, Long Walk of the Navajo, Apache Wars, Skirmish between 1st Cavalry and Indians, Snake War, Utah's Black Hawk War, Red Cloud's War, Comanche Wars, Franklin County War, U.S. troops occupy Nicaragua and attack Taiwan

1868 – Texas-Indian Wars, Long Walk of the Navajo, Apache Wars, Skirmish between 1st Cavalry and Indians, Snake War, Utah's Black Hawk War, Red Cloud's War, Comanche Wars, Battle of Washita River, Franklin County War

1869 – Texas-Indian Wars, Apache Wars, Skirmish between 1st Cavalry and Indians, Utah's Black Hawk War, Comanche Wars, Franklin County War

1870 – Texas-Indian Wars, Apache Wars, Skirmish between 1st Cavalry and Indians, Utah's Black Hawk War, Comanche Wars, Franklin County War

1871 – Texas-Indian Wars, Apache Wars, Skirmish between 1st Cavalry and Indians, Utah's Black Hawk War, Comanche Wars, Franklin County War, Kingsley Cave Massacre, U.S. forces invade Korea

1872 – Texas-Indian Wars, Apache Wars, Utah's Black Hawk War, Comanche Wars, Modoc War, Franklin County War

1873 – Texas-Indian Wars, Comanche Wars, Modoc War, Apache Wars, Cypress Hills Massacre, U.S. forces invade Mexico

1874 – Texas-Indian Wars, Comanche Wars, Red River War, Mason County War, U.S. forces invade Mexico

1875 – Conflict in Mexico, Texas-Indian Wars, Comanche Wars, Eastern Nevada, Mason County War, Colfax County War, U.S. forces invade Mexico

1876 – Texas-Indian Wars, Black Hills War, Mason County War, U.S. forces invade Mexico

1877 – Texas-Indian Wars, Skirmish between 1st Cavalry and Indians, Black Hills War, Nez Perce War, Mason County War, Lincoln County War, San Elizario Salt War, U.S. forces invade Mexico

1878 – Paiute Indian conflict, Bannock War, Cheyenne War, Lincoln County War, U.S. forces invade Mexico

1879 – Cheyenne War, Sheepeater Indian War, White River War, U.S. forces invade Mexico

1880 – U.S. forces invade Mexico

1881 – U.S. forces invade Mexico

1882 – U.S. forces invade Mexico

1883 – U.S. forces invade Mexico

1884 – U.S. forces invade Mexico

1885 – Apache Wars, Eastern Nevada Expedition, U.S. forces invade Mexico

1886 – Apache Wars, Pleasant Valley War, U.S. forces invade Mexico

1887 – U.S. forces invade Mexico

1888 – U.S. show of force against Haiti, U.S. forces invade Mexico

1889 – U.S. forces invade Mexico

1890 – Sioux Indian War, Skirmish between 1st Cavalry and Indians, Ghost Dance War, Wounded Knee, U.S. forces invade Mexico

1891 – Sioux Indian War, Ghost Dance War, U.S. forces invade Mexico

1892 – Johnson County War, U.S. forces invade Mexico

1893 – U.S. forces invade Mexico and Hawaii

1894 – U.S. forces invade Mexico

1895 – U.S. forces invade Mexico, Bannock Indian Disturbances

1896 – U.S. forces invade Mexico

1897 – No major war

https://www.globalresearch.ca/america-has-been-at-war-93-of-the-time-222-out-of-239-years-since-1776/5565946

In fact, a simple Google search on .19th Century Wars of the United States. reveals that the United

States was practically in a constant state of war or military conflict against Native tribes and Indigenous
peoples for a majority of the one-hundred-year period in question.
. First Seminole War (1817.1818)
. Texas Indian War (1820.1875)
. Arikara War (1823)
. Winnebago War (1827)
. Black Hawk War (1832)
. Second Seminole War (1835.1842)
. Cayuse War (1847.1855)
. Apache War (1851.1900)
. Puget Sound War (1855.1856)
. Rogue River Wars (1855.1856)
. Third Seminole War (1855.1858)
. Yakima War (1855.1858)
. Navajo Wars (1858.1866)
. Paiute War (1860)
. Yavbapachi Wars (1861.1875)
. Dakota War of 1862 (1862)
. Colorado War (1862.1865)
. Snake War (1864.1868)
. Powder River War (1865)
. Red Cloud.s War (1866.1868)
. Comanche Campaign (1867.1875)
. Modoc War (1872.1873)
. Red River War (1874.1875)
. Great Sioux War of 1876 (1876.1877)
. Buffalo Hunter.s War (1876.1877)
. Nez Pierce War (1877)
. Bannock War (1878)
. Cheyenne War (1878.1879)
. Sheepeater Indian War (1879)
. Victorio.s War (1879.1881)
. White River War (1897.1880)
. Pine Ridge Campaign (1890.1891)

. Yaqui Wars (1896.1918)
. Battle of Kelly Creek (1911)
. Bluff War (1914.1915)

Charles, Mark (2016) "The Doctrine of Discovery, War, and the Myth of America," *Leaven*: Vol. 24 : Iss. 3 , Article 9. Available at: http://digitalcommons.pepperdine.edu/leaven/vol24/iss3/9

Malcolm X said, “Plymouth Rock landed on us.” He was absolutely correct. We have to connect this demonic doctrine to everything that affects us today. Which include but are not limited to; police brutality, drug wars, stop and frisk, Jim Crow, Christian Black Codes, unjust criminal sentencing, Black and Negro synonymous to criminal, racial profiling, misnomer Black, colored, Negro, African-American etc, hood’s and ghetto’s, segregation, mass incarceration, Flint Michigan water crises, housing projects, poor education, poverty, police killings (shootings), lynching, integration, and innumerable other circumstances continue to represent a continuation of the Doctrine of Discovery. It can clearly be seen these are facts. This is one reason there appears to be no answer to the many problems that plague the Aboriginal Americans (Blacks, Negros, and African American). No one has really gotten to the root of the issues and found a common source. Now we have it. This is the third volume on the Doctrine of Discovery. Hopefully if you have read all three volumes, you can see how we were deceived and develop strategies for yourself and loved ones.

A lot of this information is very controversial. Most of it hasn’t been taught or is even known. More and more people are waking up to the fact that, not all of us came from Africa. Most of us were already here. The last thing I would like to state is, if the Africans were brought here as slaves in the numbers we are told (by the people who’ve told us numerous lies), why not just call them that?

Why all the name changing and identity changing with every census since 1790? (The first census)

The whole thing is based on fraud!

All emphasis mine.

www.ingramcontent.com/pod-product-compliance
Ingram Content Group UK Ltd.
Pitfield, Milton Keynes, MK11 3LW, UK
UKHW051135260726
13967UKWH00010B/3059